How to Publish
A Nonfiction Book for Free

Using Kindle Direct Publishing, CreateSpace, and Smashwords

By Christine John

http://www.ChristineJohnBooks.com

How to Publish a Nonfiction Book for Free Using Kindle Direct Publishing, CreateSpace, and Smashwords

Copyright © 2015 by Christine John

Email: christinejohnbooks@gmail.com
Website: www.ChristineJohnBooks.com

Front Cover Image: Courtesy of Stuart Miles at FreeDigitalPhotos.net

Disclaimer:
Although the author has made every effort to ensure that the information in this book was correct at press time, the author does not assume and hereby disclaim any liability to any party for any loss, damage, or disruption caused by errors or omissions, whether such errors or omissions result from negligence, accident, or any other cause.

Table of Contents

Introduction

Do you have a book that you want to publish but are not sure whether to use a traditional publisher or to try publishing it yourself? Are you unsure of which publishing platform to use? Trying to find the best platform for publishing a book for the first time can be very frustrating for new authors. Fortunately, this book will help you make the best decision in choosing a publisher and it will give you the essential tips you need to get through the whole process of publishing your book with ease.

In this book you will discover the difference between traditional publishing and self-publishing. You will also learn about the top three publishing platforms that many authors use to publish their books, which are Kindle Direct Publishing, CreateSpace, and Smashwords. This book will walk you through the whole process of publishing from uploading your files to designing your book cover, to writing your description and author bio.

I wrote this book because I wanted to inspire and help emerging authors to publish their books using the best and easiest publishing platforms on the internet. I chose to self-publish my first book and it was very difficult for me to format images according to formatting guidelines of Kindle Direct Publishing. I found it even more difficult to design a professional-looking book cover. I hope that this book will help you to avoid all the complications I went through to publish my first book.

This book consists of seven chapters and each chapter focuses on a particular aspect of publishing. You will discover what it means to self-publish your book and at the end of this book you will be ready to take your manuscript and publish it using the most suitable publishing platform.

So turn the page to the first chapter and let's get started!

Chapter 1: Self-Publishing Versus Traditional Publishing

New authors may not know much about self-publishing and may even think it is too difficult and time consuming to publish a book independently. They may also think that using the traditional method is their only option. However, authors who want to publish their work have many publishing platforms to choose from. Before you consider publishing your book let us examine the two most popular methods of publishing: self-publishing and traditional publishing, and the advantages and limitations of each option.

Traditional Publishing

In traditional publishing the author completes the manuscript, gets a literary agent (if it is fortunate that one can be found) and the agent writes and submits a proposal together with the manuscript to a publishing house. An editor reads it and decides whether to reject it or to publish it. If the publishing house decides to publish the book, then the author gets paid an advance on future royalties, but must sell the rights of the book to the publishing house. The house provides the funds to design, package and promote the book, print as many copies as it thinks will sell, and distributes the book to the public through bookstores or online retailers.

Self-Publishing

On the other hand, in self-publishing the author becomes the publisher. The author must edit the final draft of the manuscript and provide the necessary funds to publish the book using retailers/distributors such as Amazon, Apple, Smashwords, Barnes & Noble, Sony, and Kobo. The author is responsible for marketing, packaging and promotion of the book, setting up advertising campaigns, and creating a website to showcase the book. Previously, the author once had to decide on the number of copies to print and this sometimes led to hundreds of books being left in the garage or in the basement to collect dust. Fortunately, authors can now rely on Print on Demand technology which only prints the number of copies that they need.

Advantages of Self-Publishing Versus Traditional Publishing

Speed

If you decided to use the traditional method of publishing, it may take years for your book to be published. Because you have to pitch the manuscript to several publishing houses, it may take more than six months to get one to be interested in your work. You may have to wait a very long time for this to happen. If a publishing house decides to accept your manuscript, the whole process of producing the book may take at least another year.

With self-publishing, however, you can have your book published in less than six months. The internet has definitely increased the speed at which authors can now publish their books. You have the option to produce paperback or hardcover and you can even choose to have your work published as an e-book. Publishing an e-book can take a few minutes. It is the quickest way to get published and bring your book to market.

Control

You lose all rights to your book when you hand it over to a publishing house. The editor at the publishing house can take your manuscript and completely change it so that it meets the house's standards for publishing. You may face rejection from a traditional publisher because your book may be too controversial to be published or the publisher is of the opinion that it won't sell.

If you decide to publish a book yourself, you have much greater control over what you write about, how it is written, the appearance and cover design of the book, and where the book is marketed and distributed. You retain complete control of the entire publishing and marketing process.

Retaining Publishing Rights

Independent authors get to retain the rights to their published works. What this means is that the author can change the book's content, cover design, and formatting at any time. On the other hand, if you were to use the traditional method of publishing, the publishing house would retain the rights to your book and you would have to comply with any changes the publishing house made to your book.

Inventory

In traditional publishing, if a publishing house accepted your manuscript to publish the house would take on the expense of editing, designing, and packaging your book. The house would print out as many copies that it thinks would sell. Although your book will be sold online via websites and in bookstores, there is no guarantee that all the copies of your book will sell. Whatever copies are left will remain on the shelves of bookstores or in warehouses collecting dust.

If you self-publish your book you would not need to worry about printing thousands of copies of your book because many custom printing companies today offer Print-on-Demand publishing. What this means is that self-published authors can print copies of their books when needed. Books can be printed individually and shipped when ordered, which prevents authors from having to ship the books themselves or store any unsold books in the garage.

Decide for Yourself: Use a Traditional Publisher or Publish the Book Yourself

Having looked at self-publishing and traditional publishing, decide for yourself what's best for you. Are you willing to wait for a publishing house to accept your manuscript and pay you royalties in advance? Or do you prefer to have complete control of your book and reduce the time it takes to get your book published?

The best part about being a self-published author is that there are more options available. You have the internet, Print on Demand services, and online booksellers to distribute your book for you. You have complete control of the writing, editing, publishing and marketing of your book. There are also affordable professional services you can purchase, such as book cover designers, editors, and internet marketers that will not force you to empty your wallet to publish, package and promote your book. Decide for yourself which publishing service you want to use to publish and distribute your book.

Chapter 2: Eight Self-Publishing Mistakes and How to Avoid Them

It is so easy to self-publish a book in print and e-book formats, but while going through the whole process many authors make some common mistakes which can cause them to lose profits. The following 8 mistakes can harm your book sales and I will show you how you can avoid them.

Mistake #1: Unattractive Book Cover Design

Having an outstanding book cover is key to generating book sales. There are millions of e-books listed on Amazon, Barnes & Noble, and other online book sellers' sites that you have to create a cover that can stand out from the rest. Because your book will be displayed online in thumbnail view, you need to make sure that your title and author name are clear for people to read and that the images on the cover are recognizable. You can design the cover yourself but it is better to get a professional to design the cover for you. Before you upload your image make sure that you preview your cover in a small size such as 150 pixels width.

Mistake #2: Boring Title

In order to generate book sales you need to have an attention-grabbing title. Your book will be competing with other similar titles and you need to make your book more attractive than the rest. If the title of your book does not clearly tell the reader what your book is about, then you can be sure that they will not find your book. The best way to help readers find your book is to use popular keywords in the title. Go to Google Keyword Planner and look up the best keywords people use to search for your particular topic. Then use the most searched for terms in your title and this will help to boost sales of your book.

Mistake #3: Lack of Editing

Nobody wants to read a book containing grammatical errors and misspelled words. These errors can lead to bad reviews and a significant decrease in book sales. Before you publish your book, make sure that you edit its content. You can either do the editing yourself, get a family member or a close friend to proofread it for you, or, if you can afford it, hire a professional editor and proof reader.

Mistake #4: Weak Book Description

Writing a book description is something that many authors find difficult to do. The book description will be displayed next to your book cover and if it does not convince readers to buy your book than the consequences can be damaging. You need to write a compelling description to persuade your potential readers that your book is worth purchasing. In order to capture the attention of your readers you can hire a professional copy editor to write the description for you or you can search online for the best way to write a compelling book description.

Mistake #5: Neglecting Your Author Bio

Many authors make the mistake of leaving out the author biography when they self-publish their books. Skipping your author bio can leave a bad impression on your potential readers. If you want people to buy your book, show them who you are and why they should buy your book. The author bio is the perfect place to establish yourself as an authority on a particular topic and this helps readers to know who you are. If you need help writing the best author bio, check out author bios of your competition to get some ideas. You can also look up articles online that teach you how to write the best author bio.

Mistake #6: Putting too Much Unnecessary Information at the Front of Your Book

When you self-publish a book, it is tempting to include dedication, acknowledgements, book reviews, prologue and a section about the author, but this can damage your chances of selling your book. When a potential reader downloads a sample of your book this is what they will read first. They will not be able to read your actual book because you have stuffed the first few pages with unnecessary information. I know that you want to thank all the people who contributed to the creation of your book, but you can do this by putting all that extra information at the back of your book. Make sure that your readers can sample as much of your book as possible so that they will want to buy your book.

Mistake #7: Lack of Marketing

Your book sales depend on your efforts in marketing your book. Nobody is going to find your book if you don't promote it. In order to generate book sales, you need to create a website and blog on topics relevant to your book. You can also promote your book through social media and submit your title to book listing sites such as Author Marketing Club, Freebooksy, and Awesome Gang.

Mistake #8: Using Other People's Quotes or Lyrics in Your Book Without Permission

Many first time authors think that just because it is displayed online for the world to see that they can use snippets of someone else's content in their books. Unfortunately, using other people's words, photos, or paintings without permission can cost you a lot of money and can be damaging to the success of your book. Any creative expression such as music, poetry, and photos are protected by copyright law, and violations of this law can be very expensive and can damage your reputation. To avoid making this mistake, always get permission first from the owner of the copyright.

Keep these self-publishing tips in mind when writing and publishing your book. Ensure that you avoid these mistakes and you will be a successful author.

Chapter 3: Choose Your Publisher

Congratulations! Now that you have polished your e-book to saleable standards you are now ready to publish it. In order for this to happen, you first need to choose your platform and then convert the text into a format that is suitable for publishing.

Gone are the days when you had to go through the traditional way of publishing. Years ago, if you wanted your book in print you would have had to try to hire a literary agent or write a proposal to a large publishing company. Now, thanks to the various online publishing platforms like Amazon KDP, CreateSpace and Smashwords, you don't have to approach any of those giant publishing houses. Instead, you can now publish your own e-book through the process of self-publishing.

When you self-publish, this simply means that you the author will be publishing your own e-book independently without the help of an established third-party publisher. Fortunately, most online publishing platforms allow you to publish your e-book for free.

There are several options that are now available online that you can use to publish your e-book, but we will focus on two of the most popular free publishing platforms: Amazon KDP and Smashwords.

Publishing Your Book Using Kindle Direct Publishing

Kindle Direct Publishing (KDP) is an independent publishing service owned by Amazon which helps first time as well as established authors to publish and distribute their books to millions of readers worldwide. It is free to publish your book to Kindle and best of all, you keep control of your work.

With KDP, you can publish your e-book very quickly. It only takes a few minutes to publish your e-book and it will appear on Amazon sites within a couple of days. Additionally, you can earn up to 70% in royalties for sales to customers in the US, UK, Australia, Germany, and many other countries. Furthermore, because your e-book will be sold worldwide, you also have the option to publish your work in different languages. Amazon also has specialized reading apps and devices called Kindles. If you decide to use the KDP platform to publish your e-book then it will be made available for all Kindle devices and free Kindle reading apps.

After you publish your e-book to Amazon's Kindle Store, Amazon starts to promote your e-book right away on their websites. Amazon promotes your e-book to customers in various areas of their website such as:

1. "More items to consider"
2. "Customers with similar searches purchased"
3. "Customers who bought this item also bought"
4. Shopping cart recommendations "Frequently Bought Together"

Amazon also allows you to set up your own Author page to list your books as well. Go to <u>Amazon Author Central</u> to create your Author page.

There are other ways to promote your e-book on Amazon. There are several promotional tools you can use if you enrol your book in the KDP Select Program. You can use Kindle Countdown Deals to set a limited-time discount with a countdown timer to call attention to your e-book title. Kindle Matchbook is another promotional tool which allows customers who purchased other editions of your book can buy your Kindle edition at a reduced price. Additionally, you can also set free e-book promotions in which you can make your e-book available for free for a limited time.

There is also Kindle Pre-Order which allows customers to order your e-book as early as 90 days before your book's release date. You can purchase advertising to promote your e-books that are enrolled in the KDP Select program.

Although Amazon offers all these amazing benefits, there are some drawbacks to using this independent publishing platform. One is that you are limited to publishing only to the Kindle store. Amazon does not distribute your e-book to any other sites except its own stores. Secondly, although Amazon pays royalties you are limited to 70% royalty if you set the price of your e-book between $2.99 and $9.99 and 35% royalty if your price is set from $0.99 to $200.00. You can learn more about KDP's List Price Requirements by visiting their website.

Now that you know more about self-publishing your book through Kindle Direct Publishing, the following are step-by-step instructions on how to publish your own book using KDP.

1. Go to Amazon.com or Amazon.co.uk and scroll down to the bottom.
2. Under the heading **Make Money with Us** click on the link Independently Publish with Us and click **Sign Up** to create your account. You can use either your existing Amazon account or create a new one.
3. You will be required to provide additional information such as your banking details so that Amazon can wire your royalties to your account. Initially, authors were paid on a quarterly basis, but now Amazon pays royalties every month.
4. Once you have created your account, Amazon takes you to the Kindle dashboard. This is where you can add new titles of your books and check out reports on book sales from all of Amazon's websites.
5. If your book is ready to be published click **Create New Title**.
6. Enter your book details in the text boxes provided. You will need to enter the title of your book and a subtitle if it

has one. If it doesn't have a subtitle, leave the text box blank.

7. Check the box if your book is part of a series. If your book is a first edition then enter number '1'.

8. Next, enter the name of your publisher if you have one. If you are the publisher then you can enter your own name or leave this section blank.

9. Type in the description of your book. This will be shown on your book's sales page when it is published.

10. Click **Add Contributors** and type in the names of the author and any additional contributors to your book if there are any.

11. Select what language your book is in. If you have an ISBN number, make sure to enter the correct number in the text box. If you don't have an ISBN number, leave it blank. You don't need one when publishing your book using KDP. Amazon will assign an ASIN number to your book instead.

12. Next, verify your publishing rights. Select whether or not your book is a public domain work. If your book is in the public domain in one country and not in any other country, you need to identify your territory rights. I personally

recommend that you publish your own work which you hold the necessary publishing rights to.

13. The next step is to target your book to customers by selecting the appropriate category. Amazon allows you to add two categories for your book. If you need help choosing the right category then search Amazon for books that are similar to yours. Click on a book and if you scroll down the details page, you will find the categories selected for that book where it says **Amazon Bestsellers Rank**. If you cannot find the right category for your book, email Amazon and ask for a particular category.

14. Select minimum and maximum age range if you have written a book for children and select the US Grade Range to help readers find books that are suitable for a child's reading level.

15. Next, enter your best keywords that readers might use to find your book. For example, if you wrote a book about gardening, the keywords you could include are home gardening, organic home gardening, home gardening tips, home gardening tools, new home gardening ideas, home gardening supplies, starting a home garden.

16. Select your book release option. Select whether you are ready to release your book immediately or if you would like to make it available for pre-order.

17. Next, upload or create a book cover. You can either use KDP's Cover Creator tool or upload your own book cover. You must read KDP's cover guidelines first before you upload your book cover. This will be explained later when you are ready to format your book and cover.

18. The next step is to upload your book file. Make sure that you read KDP's content guidelines first before you upload your file. Also select the option whether or not you want to enable Digital Rights Management (DRM). What this means is that if you select the option to enable DRM this prevents the unauthorized distribution of your Kindle book. On the other hand, if you choose not to enable DRM, your readers can share your Kindle book with anyone at any time.

19. Once you have uploaded your files to KDP, a message will appear saying that upload and conversion of your files was successful. Another message will appear indicating whether or not your file has any spelling errors. If there are spelling errors found in your book file, simply make corrections to your file and re-upload it.

20. The next step is to preview your book. You can do this two ways: you can preview your book online or download Amazon's previewer tool. The easiest way is to preview your content online. The online previewer tool allows you to preview your book as it will appear on various Kindle e-readers and on iPad and iPhone. If you want to download the previewer tool click on the link 'Download Book Preview File', and follow the instructions on how to open your book in the previewer tool.

21. When you have fully completed the book details page, click the orange button **Save and Continue.**

22. In this step you need to set your publishing rights and the pricing of your book. First you need to verify your publishing territories. Select the Worldwide Rights option if you hold the rights to your book in all territories. If you hold rights to a certain number of territories then you need to click on the option of Individual Territories and select all the territories in the list below where you hold rights to your book.

23. Next, you need to set the price and royalty of your book. First, select a royalty option for your book and enter the list price in the table next to Amazon.com. If you select 35% royalty, this means that you can price your book

between $0.99 and $200.00 and you will receive 35% of the list price you set for your book. On the other hand, if you select 70% royalty, then you have to set your book's list price between $2.99 and $9.99. You will earn 70% royalty on the list price of your book. The Estimated Royalty in the last column shows the estimated amount of royalty you would earn based on your list price and the royalty option you selected.

24. You can choose to enrol your book in the Kindle Matchbook program. This program allows customers who purchased your print book (that is, if you have published a book in print format) the opportunity to also purchase your Kindle book for $2.99 or less.

25. Under Kindle Book Lending, select whether you will allow lending for your book. If you allow lending, this means that people can share your book with anyone at any time.

26. Click the check box indicating that you have all the rights necessary to make your book available for sale and distribution in all the territories you selected and that you are in compliance with the KDP terms and conditions.

27. And finally, click the orange button **Save and Publish.**

It seems like a lot of work, but Kindle Direct Publishing is, in my humble opinion, the easiest and fastest way to get your book published in Kindle (e-book) format. Just follow the instructions step by step and you will have your book published and listed on Amazon's website in 12 hours.

Publishing Your Book Using CreateSpace

CreateSpace is a publishing platform that you can use to publish your book in print format. CreateSpace offers free tools as well as professional services which makes it easy to publish and distribute your book. The free tools include templates to set up your book's interior, book cover templates, and an online reviewer tool. When you publish with CreateSpace you don't have to worry about printing copies of your book or shipping it yourself to customers. This publishing platform offers Print-on-Demand service which means they only print books when customers order and they take care of processing payments and shipping your book.

In order for you to publish your book in print, you are required to assign an ISBN number to your book. Fortunately, CreateSpace gives you four options to choose from to do this, including an offer of a free ISBN number which they assign.

Included with your free membership is that CreateSpace allows you to upload your book to Amazon, which makes your book available on Amazon.com and Amazon's European websites. Additionally, CreateSpace allows you to expand your distribution to bookstores, online retailers, and libraries within the United States.

Every time your book is printed and distributed to a new customer you earn royalties. CreateSpace calculates royalties based on the list price you set for your book. This gives you the freedom to choose your own royalty rate. You get to choose your royalty payment option in local currencies including US dollars (USD), British Pounds (GBP), and Euro (EUR).

Unfortunately, the way CreateSpace calculates royalties can be a bit difficult to understand. If you go to CreateSpace.com, you can find more information about how your royalty payment is calculated. CreateSpace subtracts their share from your list price to determine the royalty you earn. CreateSpace's share is comprised of the percentage of the list price for each sales channel, the fixed charge and per page charge based on the print location.

Therefore, the formula for calculating your royalties is as follows: List Price (set by you) – CreateSpace's Share = Your Royalty CreateSpace's Share = Sales Channel % + Fixed Charge + Per Page Charge

You can find all the information about how your royalty is calculated and how CreateSpace's share is calculated by visiting the CreateSpace.com website.

The following steps will help you to start the process of publishing your book using CreateSpace.

1. Go to www.createspace.com and click the blue **Sign Up** button.
2. Enter your email address, password, and your first and last name, choose your country, choose 'book' for the type of media you are considering publishing, and then click **'Create My Account'**. Then follow the instructions to get your book published.

3. When you open a new account you will receive an ID number and when you sign in, the page opens to the Member Dashboard. On the dashboard, click the blue button **Add New Title**.

4. You will be taken to the Start New Project page. On this page, you will begin the process of publishing your book. Enter the name of your book in the text box provided, the type of project, and choose a setup process.

5. CreateSpace gives you two options which you can choose to publish your book. The **Guided** process consists of step-by-step instructions to help you with publishing your book. I recommend selecting this option if this is the first time you are using CreateSpace to publish your book. Although I have used this publishing platform many times, this is still the option I choose because it is easy to follow. The **Expert** process, on the other hand is for more experienced authors who are familiar with the whole process of publishing a book with CreateSpace. Click the blue **Get Started** button next to the option you chose to start the process.

6. On the Title Information page, enter the title of your book, subtitle, name of author, contributors (if there's any), and series name and number (if applicable), select the language

your book is written in and enter the publication date. Click **Save and Continue.**

7. Next, you need an ISBN number in order to publish and distribute your book. CreateSpace gives you four options to choose from; the first option is free. If you are a first time author and you don't have an ISBN number, CreateSpace will assign an ISBN number to your book at no charge. This is the option I always choose. Please ensure that you choose the option that is suitable for you because once you make your choice it cannot be changed. When you have completed this section, click **Continue**.

8. In the next step, we will be focusing on the interior of your book. Under Interior Type, choose the colour of your text, whether it will be printed in black & white or colour. You also need to choose whether the colour of the paper will be in white or cream. Additionally, you need to choose the trim size of your book. The most popular trim size is 6"x9", but you can choose any paperback size. CreateSpace provides formatted templates created in Microsoft Word, but I don't use them because I found it very difficult to format text when I copied and pasted my files in the template. I more prefer to change the margins and trim size of the book myself. Later I will show you

how to set the trim size and format your file before you upload it to CreateSpace.

9. After you have formatted your book in accordance to the formatting guidelines provided by CreateSpace, the next thing you need to do is upload your book file. Click on the blue **Browse** button, select your book file and click **OK**. Your manuscript will go through the CreateSpace automated print check. You can view your book page by page using the Interior Reviewer. If there are any formatting errors, you will find them in the Interior Reviewer. Unfortunately, you will have to fix them and then re-upload your file. It may be time consuming, but it's worth it.

10. The next step is to design your book cover. First, choose either matte or a glossy finish for your book cover. For my books, I always choose glossy. To me it just looks more professional and attractive.

11. Next, choose how you are going to submit your book cover. You can either build your cover online with CreateSpace's cover creator for free, upload a print-ready PDF cover, or hire a professional to design the cover for you. CreateSpace provides instructions on how to upload a PDF cover. If you decide to hire a professional, I suggest

that you visit Fiverr.com where you can hire a designer to create your book cover for you starting at $5.00.

12. CreateSpace's cover creator tool is very easy to use. First, choose from several pre-made cover designs or design your own cover using a blank template. Instructions on how to use CreateSpace's pre-made cover designs are provided and are very straightforward. If you decide to design your own book cover, look for an image and make sure that it has a DPI (dots per inch) of at least 300. Then position the title and the name of the author wherever you want on the page then save it as a JPEG file. You also need to design the back cover. Include a short description of what your book is about, a photo of the author (your choice), and either short review excerpts or some brief information about the author. Make sure that you leave space for the barcode and trimming. CreateSpace provides instructions about this. You also need to set up the spine. Once all this is complete, upload your files to CreateSpace.

13. Once CreateSpace has approved your book cover, you can then move on to the Complete Setup. This is where you can review your whole project from the title of your book to the design of your cover page. If there is anything you

need to change do it at this stage before you submit your files for review.

14. At the Review stage, you submit your files for CreateSpace to review. This is when CreateSpace checks your files to ensure that they are suitable for printing and cataloguing. If it passes the review, you will be asked if you want to order a proof copy of your book for your final approval. You will have to pay for the proof copy. I highly recommend that you do this because you may find some errors that you did not notice before that need to be corrected. Once you are satisfied, you can let CreateSpace go ahead and publish your print book.

15. Choose distribution channels. CreateSpace provides three standard distribution channels and also expanded distribution.

16. Set the price for your book. CreateSpace provides a built in calculator which helps you determine what your royalties would be if you set your book at a particular price.

17. Write a description for your book's sales page. Choose a BISAC category, include your author bio, select the language your book is written in, choose country of publication, enter your best search keywords, indicate

whether your book contains adult content, and if you want your book in large print.

Once you have hit the Publish button, your print book will be made available on Amazon's websites in 3 to 5 working days. But it will take 6 to 8 weeks for your book to be made available in the expanded distribution, i.e. online libraries, educational institutions, bookstores, etc.

Publishing Your Book Using Smashwords

Smashwords is another publishing platform that you can use to publish your e-book. You can publish your e-book for free at this website and you don't have to worry about trying to distribute it to multiple online retailers. Smashwords does all that for you, considering that they are the world's largest independent e-book distributor.

Your e-books will be distributed around the world to Apple iBooks, Barnes & Noble, Kobo, Overdrive (over 20,000 libraries), Flipkart (largest book seller in India), Oyster, Scribd, Baker & Tayler, and Page Foundry. Unlike Amazon's Kindle Direct

Publishing, you are not limited to having your e-book sold by one online book retailer.

When you publish your e-book on Smashwords, you can earn 60% in royalties from book sales which are paid by major e-book retailers and 85% in net sales from Smashwords, whereas Amazon only pays up to 70% in royalties.

Smashwords also offers special promotions for authors so that you can increase sales of your e-book. As soon as you publish your e-book you can participate in the following promotions:

1. Read an E-book Week
2. Smashwords Summer/Winter Sale
3. Smashwords Coupon Manager
4. Smashwords Series Manager
5. Smashwords Interviews

The great thing about using Smashwords is that they provide easy step-by-step instructions that help you to create, publish and distribute your e-book. They provide free ISBN numbers to include in your e-book, or you can use your own. You can convert your e-book for free from a Word document to multiple formats such as mobi, epub, etc. Additionally, you get free unlimited anytime updates to your e-book and free consolidated sales reporting that simplifies year-end tax reporting.

It is very easy to get started publishing on Smashwords.

1. Go to www.Smashwords.com and sign up for your free account.

2. Read the Smashwords Terms of Service. The terms of service simply informs authors and publishers that Smashwords is a distributor of e-books. So any work that is uploaded to Smashwords is owned solely by the auhor/publisher.

3. Read the Smashwords Frequently Asked Questions (FAQ). If you think of any questions while in the process of publishing your book, you can check out the FAQ's to find the solution to a problem you may be experiencing in the whole publishing process.

4. Next, download the **Smashwords Style Guide** which gives you instructions on how to format your e-book in Microsoft Word before you upload it.

5. If you are publishing a book for the first time, click on the "Publish" menu in the blue bar.

6. Enter the title of your book in the text box provided. Remember to capitalise the first letter of each word, e.g. WordPress for Beginners.

7. Enter a short description of your book. Your description must be less than 400 characters. You could type out your description in Microsoft Word. To check the number of characters you have used, click on the **Review** tab if you are using Microsoft Office 2010 or 360, and click **Word Count**. Or you can see the word count at a glance by checking out the word count on the status bar on the bottom left of the page.

8. The next step is to set the language of the book and to state whether your book contains adult content. Select the 'My book contains adult content' button if your book has adult content.

9. Select a pricing option and allow sampling of your book. What this means is that readers will be allowed to read part of your book for free. Make sure that you choose what percentage of your book you want people to read before they purchase it.

10. Next, select two categories for your book. For example, if your book is about designing websites then you may

choose the Web Marketing category and the Web Designing category.

11. Smashwords allows you to add tags so that people may be able to find your book. Make sure that you use tags that are relevant to the topic you have written about. You are only allowed to enter a maximum of 10 tags.

12. Upload an image of your book cover to Smashwords. The maximum size of your image must be 50MB. The image is used as a thumbnail for your ebook and is inserted automatically into the ePub and mobi formats. Requirements for the cover image can be found in the Smashwords Style Guide.

13. Upload your manuscript to Smashwords. You are required to upload an MS Word document and its maximum size must be 10MB.

14. And then the final step is to publish your e-book.

If there are no errors found in your e-book or with your cover image, Smashwords will distribute your e-book to other online book retailers such as Apple, Kobi, Barnes & Noble, etc.

Chapter 4: Format Your Book for Publication

Once you have chosen the publishing platform that you will use to publish your e-book, the next thing you have to do is to format your e-book so that it will be ready for upload. The formatting guidelines for Amazon KDP are very straightforward and you can have your e-book ready in a few minutes. But including images in your e-book can be a little tricky and if you don't do it right, the images will not show when your e-book is published.

Smashwords, on the other hand, requires that you follow their style guide because you will be converting your e-book to multiple formats from your Word document. Formatting your e-book using the Smashwords method may take a little bit longer, but the advantage is that you will be able to distribute your e-book to other online retailers in various formats. By doing it this way you gain wider exposure of your e-book.

Unlike Kindle Direct Publishing and Smashwords, CreateSpace involves publishing your book in print format. If you choose to publish your book using CreateSpace, formatting your book will be a bit different. Formatting involves changing the margins of your Word document, saving it as a PDF file, and designing the front, spine and back cover of your book. You also have to make sure that the images in your book are printable, meaning that the images should come out clear when the book is printed. Publishing your book to CreateSpace is a great way to get a physical copy of your book. (Personally, it makes me feel more like an author when I see my books in print.)

Formatting Guidelines for Kindle Direct Publishing

Kindle Direct Publishing has a Simplified Formatting Guide that shows you how to format your e-book so that it will be ready to be published. Make sure that you follow these guidelines so that the text within your e-book is readable and that the images are visible and clear for your readers to view.

When creating your e-book make sure that you write it in Microsoft Word because it is very easy to format. You are now able to insert tables into your document and you can also indent paragraphs, make your text bold or in italics, and headings.

Unfortunately, you cannot use any special fonts, headers and footers, or bullet points within your document.

At the end of every chapter insert a page break so that your text does not run together. You can also insert images in JPEG (.jpeg) format and align them in the centre of your document. Do not copy and paste your images because they will not be visible when you publish your content. Instead, in your Word document, select **Insert** tab at the top and click on **Pictures**. Choose an image from the relevant folder and click **Insert**. Check out KDP's **Image Formatting Guide** for more help in formatting images.

Don't forget to use Spellcheck and Grammar to check for any misspellings and typos in your document. You should also proofread your work to ensure that no errors are missed by the automatic checker.

At the front of your e-book, you need to include a Title page and a Copyright page. It is optional if you decide to include a Dedication, Preface, and Prologue. Ensure that your e-book has an active Table of Contents that allows readers to easily navigate your e-book. Once you have completed the formatting of your e-book and are satisfied with the results, save your work in **Web**

Page, Filtered format. Your Word document will be converted to HTML and will be ready to be uploaded to KDP.

Upload your e-book cover which will be added automatically to your book file when you go through the process of publishing your e-book.

Once you have followed all of the instructions and filled in the details in KDP, click **Save** and **Publish**. Your book will appear for sale on the Amazon US Kindle Store in approximately 12 hours. In 48 to 72 hours, the book image and description will appear in all the other Amazon stores worldwide.

How to Format Images Within Your Kindle Book

Adding images to your Kindle e-book can be very challenging. Your image has to be a certain size and of a particular file type for it to be viewed on a Kindle or e-book reading device. Fortunately, Amazon KDP has provided an Image Formatting Guide that explains how to format images within your Kindle e-book.

Kindle Direct Publishing accepts images in JPEG (.jpeg) format and the maximum size of JPEG interior image files is up to 5MB.

If you have inserted images into your Microsoft Word document, Kindle Direct Publishing extracts images from your file and replaces them with HTML <img> tags. This is what happens when you save your Word document as an HTML file (Web Page, filtered). Each image is converted into a separate image file, which becomes a part of your e-book's publication package.

Take note that when you preview your uploaded file, the images in your e-book will not be displayed accurately. For example, larger images may resize or rotate when previewed. Based on my own experience, you may not even see the images that you inserted into your Word document. They may all appear as a camera in place of where the image should have been.

Kindle e-Book Cover Specifications

The cover of your e-book will be uploaded separately from the e-book itself. Amazon KDP accepts only two types of files for book cover images: JPEG and TIFF and the size of the file must be less than 50MB. The file must also be saved with 72 dots per inch (dpi).

KDP also requires that your cover image must be of a particular size, i.e. a minimum of 625 pixels on the shortest side (width) and 1000 pixels on the longest side (height). For best quality, you can increase the height to 2500 pixels, but your image must not be any larger than 10,000 pixels on the longest side.

Now this may seem difficult at first because you may not know how to resize your image to meet KDP's size specifications, but there is a very easy way to get this done without using complicated software like Photoshop or hiring an expensive image editor. You can simply use Paint, a free program which is already installed on your computer.

How to Resize an Image Using Paint

First, go to the folder where you saved your e-book cover image. Right click on the image and select **Edit**. The image opens in the Paint program. On the **Home** tab in the **Image** group click **Resize**. In the **Resize and Skew** dialog box ensure that the **Maintain**

Aspect Ratio check box is selected. When the Maintain Aspect Ratio check box is selected, you only need to enter the horizontal value (width) or vertical value (height). The other box in the **Resize** area is updated automatically.

To resize the image so that it is a specific size, click **Pixels** in the **Resize** area and then enter a new width in the horizontal box or a new height in the vertical box.

For example, change the width in the horizontal box to 625 pixels, or change the height in the vertical box to 1000 pixels. It doesn't matter which one you change, the other will be updated automatically.

When you are satisfied with the size of your image, click the **File** tab and click **Save As**. Select the required file type (I highly recommend JPEG), choose the folder where you want to save the file and then click **Save**. Now you can upload your image to KDP. Log in to your KDP account and follow the instructions to upload your cover image.

Formatting Guidelines for CreateSpace

Once you have set up an account with CreateSpace, you are now ready to publish your book in print format. This website provides step-by-step easy to follow instructions on how to publish your book.

The first part of the publishing process is to setup your book. In this section you provide the title of your book, name of author and the ISBN number. I mentioned above that you can get a free ISBN number from CreateSpace to use in your book. Next, you need to format the interior of your book which must meet the requirements of CreateSpace in order to publish your book without any complications. You need to set the trim size of your book and the margins, according to the number of pages that will be printed. You can do all this using Microsoft Word.

Before you upload your file to be published, CreateSpace has submission requirements which you must follow or else your manuscript will be rejected. One of the submission requirements is that your book must be of a particular trim size. The trim size is basically the size of the pages of your book. The table below lists the trim sizes that CreateSpace will accept. Trim sizes are measured in both inches (") and centimetres (cm).

Trim Sizes of Books Accepted by Createspace

Width: 5" Height: 8"	Width: 5.06" Height: 7.81"	Width: 5.25" Height: 8"
Width: 6" Height: 9"	Width: 6.14" Height: 9.21"	Width: 6.69" Height: 9.61"
Width: 7.44" Height: 9.69"	Width: 7.5" Height: 9.25"	Width: 8" Height: 10"
Width: 8.25" Height: 8.25"	Width: 8.5" Height: 8.5"	Width: 8.5" Height: 11"
Width: 5.5" Height: 8.5"	Width: 7" Height: 10"	Width: 8.25" Height: 6"

To ensure that your book has the correct trim size, you will need to edit your file in Microsoft Word. Use the **Page Layout** tab in Word to format your manuscript.

For example:

1. Click on **Page Layout** tab in Microsoft Word.
2. Click on the arrow under **Size**.
3. Select **More Paper Sizes**.

4. Under **Paper Sizes**, enter the **Width** and **Height**.

5. Under **Preview**, make sure that **Whole Document** is selected where it says **Apply to**.

Page Layout – Size – More Paper Sizes

Width: 6" (15.2cm)

Height: 9" (22.9cm)

Apply to: Whole document

Images or Elements that Bleed

If you have any images that bleed you will need to adjust the width and height of the pages of your book. Bleed simply means that you have images that extend all the way to the edges of a page. Add 0.125" (0.3cm) to the Width and 0.25"(0.6cm) to the Height if you have images that bleed. For example, for the trim size of 6" x 9" (15.2cm x 22.9cm) plus bleed, you will change the paper size to 6.125" x 9.25" (15.6cm x 23.5cm).

Margins

1. Under the **Page Layout** tab, click on the arrow under **Margins** and select **Custom Margins**.

2. Adjust the size of your margins based on the submission requirements and the number of pages your book contains. Next to **Multiple Pages** in the **Pages** area, select **Mirror Margins**. Two pages appear mirroring each other in the **Preview** area. When you open a book the margins should mirror each other.

3. The **Gutter Margin** is the area in the spine/binding region of an open book. Set the gutter margin based on your page count. For example, for a 120-page book the gutter margin should be at least 0.375" (1cm).

4. The **Inside Margin** is the same as the gutter margin. Set the inside margin to 0".

5. The **Top, Bottom**, and **Outside Margins** should all be the same size. Enter 0.5" (1.3cm) for these margins.

The requirements for the Gutter Margin are listed below:

24 to 150 pages: 0.375" (1cm)

151 to 400 pages: 0.75" (1.9cm)

401 to 600 pages: 0.875" (2.2cm)

More than 600 pages: 1.0" (2.5cm)

CreateSpace also allows you to insert headers, footers, drop caps and indent paragraphs in your manuscript. Click on the **Insert** tab to insert page breaks, page numbers, headers, footers and drop caps. Make sure that you add page numbers and headers before you start typing your book.

You can also make changes to the layout of your text. Click on the **Home** tab and in the Paragraph section click on the arrow in the corner. You can change the indentation of the first line of each paragraph and change the spacing between paragraphs. Additionally, select the option in the Paragraph section to justify text to make each line begin and end in the same position.

It would be very beneficial to you if you read "A Step-by-Step Guide to Formatting Your Book's Interior". This article gives you instructions on how to format the interior of your book. Once you are satisfied with the format of your book's interior, save it as a PDF document and upload it to CreateSpace.

The next thing you need to take care of is your book cover. You can choose a template provided by CreateSpace to design your book cover or you can upload your own image. Be sure to follow CreateSpace's guidelines on designing your book cover.

When you have uploaded your book's interior file and designed the cover page, your files will then be sent for review to ensure that its pages are suitable for printing. You can review your book online by using CreateSpace's free reviewer tool. Once your files have been approved you can order a proof copy of your book so that you will see how it will look in print before it is actually published. This would be the best time to check over your work to ensure that there are no spelling mistakes, grammatical errors, and that any images you included in your book are printed clearly.

The next section involves the distribution of your book. CreateSpace offers six sales channels where you can distribute your book. The standard distribution channels are Amazon.com, Amazon Europe, and the CreateSpace eStore. The other channels are known as Expanded Distribution, which include bookstores and online retailers, libraries and academic institutions, and CreateSpace Direct. You can choose to stick with just the standard distribution channels or you can select the expanded distribution channels as well. It's your choice.

Formatting Guidelines for Smashwords

The first thing you need to do before you format your e-book for Smashwords is to download the **Smashwords Style Guide**. The process of formatting your e-book in this case is much longer than what you would do for Amazon KDP. But the steps in the Style Guide are very detailed with pictures to show you exactly what to do.

Instructions for formatting your e-book is too long to include in this book, but here are a few main points that you need to do to prepare your book for publishing on Smashwords. First, it is highly recommended that you should write your e-book in Microsoft Word. You should also back up your file before you make any changes to it. In other words, do not try to format the original document. Instead create a copy of it.

Next you need to clean up your Word document before you actually format it. Activate Word's Show/Hide to reveal your hidden formatting. Turn off Word's AutoCorrect and AutoFormat features. Turn off Track Changes. Use the Nuclear Method to purge hidden corruption.

The next step is to format your content. Change the Paragraph style of your text to Normal. You will also need to change the way you indent the first line of your paragraphs. You will find special tips for formatting the content of fiction, poetry, cookbooks and learning materials. You also need to define proper line spacing of your text. The style guide will also show you how to avoid common line spacing errors.

The style guide also shows you how to manage font colour of your text and how to make your text bold, italic and underlined. You will also learn how to change the front matter of your document, i.e. the title, name of the author, copyright page, and license statement of your book. Additionally, the style guide shows you how to automate the removal of tabs and space bar spaces.

There are some things that you are not allowed to include in your book. Smashwords does not allow you to include affiliate links, competitive retailer links, or PDFs. You will be in violation of Smashwords' Terms of Service and your account may be closed if affiliate links are found in your book. You can link to your author profile on Smashwords, but it is inconsiderate to include links to other competitive e-book retailers. Your book should not be used as an advertising vehicle for other retailers. You also should not include links to PDF documents because not all e-reading devices support PDF documents.

The Smashwords Style Guide will show you how to designate page breaks, section breaks and chapter breaks. You are allowed to insert images into your document but it is advised that you insert only .JPEG or .PNG images. The file upload limit of your Word document must be less than 10 MB. If it is greater than that you can make the file smaller by compressing the images in your document. The style guide will show you how.

You cannot include headers and footers in your document because this will not show in e-reading devices. You should also remove auto-page numbering because this may cause a text box error.

You can change the margins, page sizes and indents of the text in your document. You can also add heading styles to your chapter headings but you have to be careful that you do not use this formatting style too often in your document. This can cause a major formatting error and make your document difficult to read.

The Smashwords Style Guide will show you how to build navigation into your book. It describes three ways to navigate by first creating an NCX (Navigation Control) File, creating a hyperlinked Table of Contents, and adding footnotes and endnotes in your document.

You can also create end matter that goes at the back of your book. You can include a personal note from the author requesting the reader to leave a positive review of your book, include other titles written by the author, and add links to your profile on all of your social media networks. This brings you to the end of formatting your e-book.

All you have left to do is design a professional-looking cover image and upload your book onto the Smashwords website. The Smashwords Style Guide will explain how to do this.

In the next chapter we will be looking at setting the price of your e-book.

Chapter 5: Set the Price of Your Book

Setting the price of your e-book can be a very tricky business. You want to make sure that you choose a price that is not too low that you can't make a profit, but not too high that people will not buy it. Fortunately, at both Amazon KDP and Smashwords, the author is allowed to set the price of their own books. The price is usually determined by the amount of royalty the author will receive from their book sales. Amazon KDP and Smashwords both have different policies on how royalties are paid to self-published authors.

Set the Price for Kindle Direct Publishing

Once you have uploaded your e-book to Kindle Direct Publishing, you will then be given two options of how you would like to be paid in royalties. In other words, the royalty offered by KDP is the profit you make on each sale of your e-books. You can choose either to make 70% royalty or 35% royalty, but this all depends on how you price your e-book.

For example, if you choose to make 70% royalty on each of your e-books, then you would be required to price your e-books between $2.99 and $9.99. If you prefer the 35% royalty option, then you can set the price between $0.99 and $200.00.

Set the Price for CreateSpace

As I mentioned before, you can determine how much you earn in royalties by setting your own list price. You can set your list price in US dollars (USD), British Pound (GBP) and Euro (EUR). Your royalties are calculated by subtracting CreateSpace's share from your list price. Unlike Kindle Direct Publishing and Smashwords, CreateSpace does not pay a particular percentage of the list price of your book when a customer purchases it.

The way CreateSpace calculates your royalties depends on a number of factors such as the sales channel your book is sold through, fixed charges depending on your book's page count and whether your book's interior is black and white or full colour, and per-page charge for books that have higher page counts.

The following is an example of how CreateSpace calculates royalties for your book.

CreateSpace's Share = Sales Channel % + Fixed Charge + Per Page Charge
List Price (set by you) – CreateSpace's Share = Your Royalty

Your book, for example, contains 200 pages and its interior is black and white. You set your USD list price at $7.99. A customer purchases your book from Amazon.com and your book is printed and shipped to that customer.

List Price - $7.99

Sales Channel – Amazon.com (standard distribution) 40% of list price

Fixed Charges – Black and white books with 110-828 pages: $0.85 per book

Per-page Charge – Black and white books with 110-828 pages: $0.012 per page

CreateSpace's Share = Sales Channel % + Fixed Charge + Per Page Charge

CreateSpace's Share = ($7.99 x 40%) + $0.85 + ($0.012 x 200 pages)

$$= 3.20 + 0.85 + 2.4$$
$$= \$6.45$$

Your Royalty = List Price (set by you) – CreateSpace's Share

Your Royalty = $7.99 - $6.45

$$= \$1.54$$

Therefore, the royalty you would earn for each book you sell is $1.54.

If you want to earn higher royalties then you need to set the price higher. But make sure that you do not set your price too high because you might drive away your customers and they will look for a book similar to yours at a more affordable price.

Set the Price for Smashwords

Unlike Amazon KDP, e-books are not sold exclusively at Smashwords. E-books are distributed to various online retailers and will therefore pay different royalty payments. If you choose to publish your e-book to Smashwords, then your e-book will be made available to a wider audience such as readers who shop for e-books at Barnes & Noble, Apple iBooks, Flipkart, Kobo, Overdrive, Oyster, Scribd, and more.

You can earn 60% of the list price of your e-book if it were listed on major e-book retailers' websites. And Smashwords would pay 85% in royalties if your e-book were listed at Smashwords.com.

How to Price Your Self-Published Book

Once the book is complete and is ready to be published, many authors ask themselves the question as to how to price their self-published book. Price setting can be a difficult task, but there are methods that you can use to help you find the right selling price for your book.

Think About the Reader

Before you set the price of your book, first think about the reader. Instead of thinking as an author and wondering how much is your book worth, consider the reader who has never read your book before. You may be a new author and the reader knows nothing about you. So ask yourself, how much is the reader willing to pay for your book?

Check Out the Competition

It is always good to compare the prices of competitive titles. But you should compare prices of books by other self-published authors rather than to compare prices with bestselling books from traditional publishers. Readers are more likely to pay a premium price of a book written by a well-known author rather than pay the high price for an unknown author. Therefore, if you are new to the world of self-publishing, I suggest that you start small.

Consider Your Genre

When determining what price to set for your book, consider comparing prices with books in your own genre. In other words, what category would you list your book under? Home and garden? Finance? Computers and Internet? You also need to consider the reader as well. Because you are writing a nonfiction book, your readers may buy less frequently as compared to fictional titles. So you can still compare your book to other self-published titles to get a more accurate picture of the market.

Set Goals

Determine how much profit you want to make from the sale of each of your books. Depending on the publishing platform you choose, you need to consider the amount of royalties you would receive from the sale of each book. Ask yourself how many books do you want to sell each month?

For example, let's say you chose to publish your book to Kindle Direct Publishing. KDP offers 35% of royalties paid if you price your book between $0.99 and $200.00. If you price your book between $2.99 and $9.99 then you would be paid 70% royalties.

If you price your book at $1.99 at 35% royalty, then you would be paid about $0.70 royalty for the sale of each book. Therefore if you sold 50 books then you would make $35.

On the other hand, if you priced your book at $2.99 at 70% royalty, then you would be paid $2.09 per sale. The amount you would make if you sold 50 books would be $104.50.

The best thing to do is to experiment with your prices. You can change the price of your book anytime so you can calculate how much profit you predict you will receive from each book sale. If you decide to give your book a low price, try it for a month to see how many books you sell and how much royalties you get paid. This will help you to determine the best price for your book and you can stick to that price once you are satisfied with the number of sales your book makes.

Chapter 6: Write a Description for Your Book

Many authors find it difficult to write an effective book description. It is so tempting to cram as much detail as possible about the book that it may leave the reader feeling confused as to what your book is actually about. Here are a few tips to keep in mind when you write your book description.

1. When writing your book description, focus on the main theme of your book. For example, what problem does the reader have that your book will solve?

2. You can list some of the benefits the reader will receive when they read your book. There is no specific length your description should be, as long as the reader understands what your book is about and how it will benefit them if they read it.

3. Always write in the present tense. Imagine if you were facing someone and they asked you what your book is about. You would not describe it to them in the past tense. You would use present tense and you need to write your

description as though you were speaking directly to the person.

4. Use power words in your book description. Words such as 'effective', 'powerful', 'proven', and 'successful' are just a few examples of power words that you can use in your description to evoke emotions in your reader. If you do a search on the internet for the keyword 'power words' you will find a massive list of words to help you with your book description.

This is a book description that I wrote for one of my books ***WordPress for Beginners: The Easy Step-by-Step Guide to Creating a Website with WordPress***:

UPDATED APRIL 2015!

Discover how easy it is to create a website using the web's most popular content management software: WordPress. This popular web design book has helped thousands of online users to build a professional-looking website.

WordPress for Beginners contains colourful images and easy-to-follow instructions on how to set up your very own website.

This is what you will learn in the WordPress for Beginners web design guide:

What is WordPress?

The Benefits of Using WordPress

What You Need to Use WordPress

Getting Started with WordPress: Register a Domain Name

Set Up Web Hosting

Install and Enter Your Website

Change the Appearance (Theme) of Your Website

Change the Settings of Your Site

Create a Post

Create a Page

Upload Media

Install Plugins

Manage Comments

Use Widgets

Optimize Your Site for the Search Engines

You don't need to know complicated CSS or HTML codes. If you are tired of struggling to build your website then grab your copy of this book today. Discover for yourself how easy it is to create a website with WordPress.

Here are a few examples of powerful book descriptions:

23 Steps to Success and Achievement by Robert J. Lumsden

Burn the Fat, Feed the Muscle by Tom Venuto

Digital Minds by WSI

The 4-Hour Work Week by Timothy Ferriss

Chapter 7: Write Your Author Bio

Some authors tend to skip this section, either because they find difficulty writing an author biography or because they may not think it is necessary. Whatever the reason is, I believe that including an author bio is very important because it helps you the author to connect with your readers. It also shows them that you have knowledge about the topic you are writing about and they get to know a few details about you.

Your bio normally appears below your book description near to the bottom of the page if you look at a book's sales page on Amazon. There are a number of items you can include in your author bio such as:

1. Your name
2. About two or three previous books you've published (you don't have to list all of them)
3. Awards (but not those you won in college)
4. Your job (only if it is relevant to the book you have written)

5. Professional qualification relevant to your book
6. Your likes, dislikes, and hobbies (but only if they are relevant to your book)
7. Where you live (name of city and country is enough)
8. If you're married and have children (but this is optional)

On the other hand, there are some things that you should not include in your author bio such as:

1. A complete biography (your bio does not need to be 10 pages long)
2. Personal statements (leave these at the end of your book or in the acknowledgements or dedication)
3. You don't need to include the year you were born or where you went to school unless it is relevant to your book

When writing your author bio, refer to yourself in the third person and keep it brief. You can start your bio by stating what makes you different from other authors who have written similar books in your genre. Write about something that makes you unique. Make sure that you include who you are trying to help with your books. In other words, identify your target audience. Next, list a few accomplishments if they are relevant to your book. You can also include any professional qualifications you may have, what are your favourite hobbies, and where you live. Don't forget to include a call to action. You need to tell your readers what to do next, which is to check out the books you have written or click on the buy now button to get instant access to your book.

The following authors have great examples of effective author bios:

Daniel Priestley, author of ***Entrepreneur Revolution***

Andrew Macarthy, author of ***500 Social Media Marketing Tips***

Debbie Shore, author of ***Sew Useful: Simple Storage Solutions for the Home***

Chapter 8: Choose Categories for Your Book

Ensuring that your book is placed in the right category can have a significant impact on your book sales. It is possible that one of the reasons that your sales are so low is that your book may not be in the proper category.

In order for your book to sell, people have to be able to find it. The only way they will find it is if your book is placed in the appropriate category. Fortunately, there is a very simple way that you can fix this. All you have to do is choose the categories that best match your book based on its content. Follow the steps below to place your book in the proper category.

1. Ensure that you know what category your book fits in. Is your book about entrepreneurship? Finance? Web designing?
2. Go to your Amazon sales page for your book (or a best-selling book similar to yours) and scroll down to the bottom to the section that says "Look for similar items by category".

3. In the categories list, copy the two categories that fit your book the best. For example, in the categories list for the number one bestselling book **The Rich Employee** by James Altucher, you would copy: **Kindle Store > Kindle eBooks > Business & Finance > Careers**, and **Kindle Store > Kindle eBooks > Business & Finance > Small Business & Entrepreneurship.**

4. Make sure you list your book as non-classifiable under KDP. In order to do this, sign in to your Amazon KDP account. On the Bookshelf page, on the right side of your book, hover your mouse over the button that has three dots next to the Promote and Advertise button. Click on **Edit Details** and scroll down to Step 3: Target Your Book to Customers. In this section change the categories to non-classifiable. Then click **Save and Continue**.

5. Contact Amazon KDP and make a request for them to put your book in whichever categories you ask. Scroll down to the very bottom of the Bookshelf page and click on **Contact Us**. Follow the instructions to make your request to Amazon KDP to change the categories of your book.

In a few days you will see a major difference in your book's ranking, possibly making Amazon's top 100 Bestsellers' List.

Conclusion

In this book we covered three different methods of publishing your book online. We looked at Kindle Direct Publishing, CreateSpace and Smashwords. These are the most popular publishing platforms that you can use to publish your book for free and they each allow you to earn a large percentage of royalties from the sale of your books. What you need to do now is to choose the best publishing platform for your book, create a new account, and start the process of publishing your book.

All too often, when people finish reading a book they tend to put it aside and forget all about what they had planned to do and why they started reading the book in the first place. Don't let this happen to you. If you want to publish your book then get started now. Once you have written your book, all you have to do is follow the guidelines for formatting and uploading your files and your book will be published in a couple of days.

If you have a message that you want to share with the world, take the next step and publish your book.

I wish you all the success in publishing your book!

If you found the information in this book helped you to publish your book, then you will definitely enjoy my third book: **How to Make Money Promoting and Selling a Nonfiction Book** *which will be coming soon to Amazon.*

Thank You

I hope that you found this guide to writing your nonfiction book to be very helpful. I want to say thank you for purchasing this book and for reading it all the way to the end.

I would be honoured if you could please leave a review for this book *How to Publish a Nonfiction Book for Free Using Kindle Direct Publishing, CreateSpace, and Smashwords* on Amazon.

If you feel that this book answered your questions as to how to publish a nonfiction book, then please do not hesitate to share it with your friends, family members and colleagues.

If you have any further questions or comments about this book or on writing in general, please contact me at the following email address:

ChristineJohnBooks@gmail.com

About the Author

"Writing books that inspire and help people to succeed."

Whether you need information about designing a website, writing a book, or finding a job, Christine provides the books that satisfy your needs.

Christine has written books on a variety of topics that help and inspire authors, bloggers, internet marketers, entrepreneurs, and job seekers. Included in the mix are books written for the entertainment and enjoyment of people who love to read romance novels, short stories and poetry. She has also written information to motivate individuals to reach their true potential and to succeed in life.

Christine enjoys inspiring and motivating people to develop themselves both personally and professionally, and to be more creative.

When she is not busy working on her next book, Christine enjoys reading, travelling, and helping young entrepreneurs to make their dreams a reality. Presently, Christine lives in the United Kingdom where she continues to share her knowledge with the world.

If you want to find out more, check out the books that Christine has published on Amazon.com or Amazon.co.uk. Also visit her website for more information at ChristineJohnBooks.com.

Connect with Christine

Facebook
https://www.facebook.com/ChristineJohnBooks

Twitter
https://twitter.com/CejohnBooks

LinkedIn
https://uk.linkedin.com/in/cejohn

Google Plus
google.com/+Christinejohnbooks77

YouTube
https://www.youtube.com/user/SpringMediaIntl

More Books by Christine John

Visit your local Amazon website to download the following books to your computer or Kindle. These books are also available in Print format. Go to Amazon to place your order now!

Nonfiction

How to Write a Nonfiction Book that Sells

WordPress for Beginners: The Easy Step by Step Guide to Creating a Website with WordPress

How to Start and Run an Online Business

How to Get the Job You Want

Fiction

Last Chance

The Runaway Bride

Short Stories for Teenagers

Poems About Life